First published in 2011
by Hodder Children's Books.

Copyright © Mick Inkpen 2011

Hodder Children's Books
338 Euston Road, London NW1 3BH

Hodder Children's Books Australia
Level 17/207 Kent Street, Sydney, NSW 2000

The right of Mick Inkpen to be identified as the author
and illustrator of this Work has been asserted by him in
accordance with the Copyright, Designs and Patents Act 1988.

A catalogue record of this book is
available from the British Library.

ISBN: 978 1 444 90266 2
10 9 8 7 6 5 4 3 2 1

Printed in China

Hodder Children's Books is a
division of Hachette Children's Books,
an Hachette UK Company
www.hachette.co.uk

Wibbly Pig has

10 balloons

But he likes
the teddy bear
balloon best.

h

Hodder
Children's
Books

A division of Hachette Children's Books

10

'Ten balloons!'
says Wibbly Pig.
'And all of them are mine!'
'Can I have one?'
says Tiny Pig.
So ten turns into. . .

Not the
teddy bear balloon.
It's my favourite.

'Nine balloons?'
says Scruffy Pig.
'And Tiny Pig's got one!
Nine balloons and one
make ten.
And that leaves me
with none!'

Alright, Scruffy Pig.
You can have one too.
But not the teddy bear
balloon.

8

'Eight balloons!'
says Spotty Pig.
'And Scruffy's got one too!'
'Alright, choose one,'
sighs Wibbly Pig.
The one he picks is. . .

...blue.

NOT the teddy bear balloon!

Wibbly Pig has
seven balloons.
But not for very long.
He's only just stopped
counting them. . .

Ding Dong!

. . .when Pig Ears
comes along.

And not just Pig Ears,
Big Pig too.
And Pig Twins,
both of them.
And someone else
he's never met,
Big Pig's sister's friend!

Thank you very much Wibbly.

6 5 4 3

So now he has to
count again.
Not **six**,
not **five**,
not **four**.
Just **three** balloons
is all he has. . .

Ding Dong!
Ding Dong!
Ding Dong!

But who's **this** at the door!

Big Pig's sister
wants one too.
'Let me have one.
Let me!'
She pouts and shouts
and stamps about.
But Wibbly
won't agree.

She flounces out.
She flounces in.
(She knows she'll get her way.)

She holds her breath,
and stares. . .
     and glares. . .

till Wibbly says. . .

'OK.'

She grabs the
strings from Wibbly.
'The pink one,
with the bow!
That's the one I want!'
she squeals.
And lets the
others go!

She lets the others go!

N**O** balloons for
Wibbly Pig.
He wants to cry.
No balloons for
Wibbly Pig,

but then, nearby. . .

. . .a little voice,
a weeny voice,
(a Tiny voice)
is squealing,
'Please get me down!
Please get me down!
I'm up here. . .

. . .on the ceiling!'

'This balloon is much too big!
You can have it, Wibbly Pig!'

Wibbly sniffs. . .
        helps Tiny down. . .
then sniffs some more. . .
        and stops.
        'Thank you Tiny Pig,'
he says.

And that. . .

                is when. . .

Wibbly Pig and Tiny Pig
sit sadly in the park.
They talk away the afternoon.
They talk until it's dark.

'No balloons,' sighs Wibbly Pig.
'And I started out with ten!
That teddy bear balloon was best.
I had three left, and then. . .'

But Tiny Pig's not listening.
He's staring at the moon.
There's something
floating past it. . .

. . .the teddy bear balloon!

'My teddy bear
balloon came back!'
says Wibbly,
with a grin...

And Tiny's grinning too
because...

. . .one came back for him!